TOP 10
FURRIEST
ANIMALS

Children's Press®
An imprint of Scholastic Inc.

BY BRENNA MALONEY

A special thank-you to the Cincinnati Zoo & Botanical Garden for their expert consultation.

Copyright © 2026 by Scholastic Inc.

All rights reserved. Published by Children's Press, an imprint of Scholastic Inc., *Publishers since 1920*. SCHOLASTIC, CHILDREN'S PRESS, and associated logos are trademarks and/or registered trademarks of Scholastic Inc.

The publisher does not have any control over and does not assume any responsibility for author or third-party websites or their content.

No part of this publication may be reproduced, stored in a retrieval system, or transmitted in any form or by any means, electronic, mechanical, photocopying, recording, or otherwise, or used to train any artificial intelligence technologies, without written permission of the publisher. For information regarding permission, write to Scholastic Inc., Attention: Permissions Department, 557 Broadway, New York, NY 10012.

Library of Congress Cataloging-in-Publication Data available

ISBN 978-1-5461-7748-7 (library binding)
ISBN 978-1-5461-7749-4 (paperback)

10 9 8 7 6 5 4 3 2 1   26 27 28 29 30

Printed in China   62
First edition, 2026

Book design by Kay Petronio

KOMONDOR

SEA OTTER

Photos ©: back cover left, 2 left: Daria Vorontsova/Getty Images; back cover right, 2 right: Gerald Corsi/Getty Images; 4 left: Tim Fitzharris/Minden Pictures; 4 right center: Andy Seliverstoff/Solent News/Shutterstock; 4 bottom right: Dgwildlife/Getty Images; 5 top left: Loloba/Getty Images; 5 top center: imageBROKER/Stefan Huwiler/Getty Images; 5 top right: Bangkokerz/Getty Images; 5 bottom left: Kevin Schafer/Getty Images; 5 bottom right: Richard Tadman/Alamy Images; 7: Andy Seliverstoff/Solent News/Shutterstock; 10 inset: scanrail/Getty Images; 11 right: Nature Picture Library/Alamy Images; 12-13: Tim Fitzharris/Minden Pictures; 12 inset: design56/Getty Images; 13 right: pilipenkoD/Getty Images; 14 inset: sweetym/Getty Images; 15 right: Cloudtail_the_Snow_Leopard/Getty Images; 16-17: Richard Tadman/Alamy Images; 16 inset: mladn61/Getty Images; 17 right: Gannet77/Getty Images; 18-19: Bangkokerz/Getty Images; 19 right: CreativeNature_nl/Getty Images; 20-21: Dgwildlife/Getty Images; 22-23: Loloba/Getty Images; 23 right: Siegfried Kuttig/imageBROKER/Shutterstock; 24 inset: Ratikova/Getty Images; 26 main: Jane Smith BluePlanetArchive.com; 26 inset: Jim Esposito Photography L.L.C./Getty Images; 27: Kevin Schafer/Getty Images; 28-29: David McGowen/Getty Images; 30 top right: Schafer/Getty Images; 30 bottom center: Gannet77/Getty Images. All other photos © Shutterstock.

CONTENTS

Fur, Fluff, and Other Stuff 4
#10: Komondor 6
Komondor Close-Up 8
#9: Luna Moth 10
#8: Arctic Fox 12
#7: Pallas's Cat 14
#6: Alpaca 16
#5: Binturong 18
#4: Musk Ox 20
#3: Silkie Chicken 22
#2: Angora Rabbit 24
#1: Sea Otter 26
Sea Otter Close-Up 28
Sizing Them Up 30
Glossary 31
Index/About the Author 32

FUR, FLUFF, AND OTHER STUFF

LUNA MOTH

KOMONDOR

MUSK OX

ARCTIC FOX

Fur is the coat of nonhuman **mammals**. There are so many furry animals in our wild world! Some are fluffy. Some are fuzzy. Some have short fur. Others have very long fur. Some have fur that changes colors.

Fur protects animals. It also keeps them warm. Fur can also help animals stay dry. It can even help animals hide. Are you ready to learn which animal is the furriest? Read on and count down from ten to one. Let's find out which animal takes the top spot!

PALLAS'S CAT

BINTURONG

SILKIE CHICKEN

SEA OTTER

ANGORA RABBIT

ALPACA

#10 KOMONDOR

FACT FILE

- **ANIMAL GROUP:** Mammal
- **HABITAT:** Farms
- **AVERAGE SIZE:** A large suitcase
- **DIET:** Omnivore

This dog's fur looks like thick, rope-like cords. The cords take more than a year to form. They are made from two layers of fur. There is a **woolly** outercoat. It twists together with a soft undercoat.

Many Komondors guard flocks of sheep. Their white fur helps them blend in with the sheep. And **predators** like wolves cannot bite through their tough coats.

FACT — Fur and hair are not the same! Fur is usually shorter and thicker. Hair is usually longer and finer.

KOMONDOR CLOSE-UP

BODY
Its strong body is slightly longer than it is tall.

TAIL
A long tail has a slight curl. It is mostly hidden by fur.

FACT
Komondors are also known as mop dogs. Can you guess why?

EYES
Its almond-shaped eyes are sometimes hidden by fur.

MUZZLE
It has a black nose and lips.

FUR
A heavy coat protects its body.

#9 LUNA MOTH

FACT FILE

- **ANIMAL GROUP:** Invertebrate
- **HABITAT:** Woodlands
- **AVERAGE SIZE:** A smartphone
- **DIET:** None (as an adult)

Fur on an insect? That is mostly true. The luna moth looks furry because it is covered in fur-like scales. This "fur" keeps the moths warm at night.

This is when they are most active. Hungry bats use sound waves to search for food. The moths' soft fur makes them harder to locate. The fur muffles sound. Their green wings help **camouflage** the moths.

FACT Adult luna moths have no mouths. They do not eat. They live for only one week.

#8 ARCTIC FOX

FACT FILE

ANIMAL GROUP: Mammal

HABITAT: Arctic tundra

AVERAGE SIZE: A backpack

DIET: Omnivore

The Arctic fox is built for cold weather. It has short legs, small ears, and thick fur. Its fur changes with the seasons. In spring and summer, its fur is brown. In winter, it's white, like snow.

This helps the fox blend in with its habitat. And it helps camouflage the fox from predators. The Arctic fox has a long, fluffy tail. It wraps its tail in front of its face. Its tail shields it from the wind and cold.

FACT The Arctic fox has fur on the bottom of its paws. This makes the fox a quieter hunter.

#7 PALLAS'S CAT

FACT FILE

ANIMAL GROUP: Mammal

HABITATS: Deserts, grasslands, rocky areas, shrublands

AVERAGE SIZE: A computer monitor

DIET: Carnivore

Pallas's cats have the thickest and longest fur of any cat. Their fur is almost twice as long on their belly and tail. The fur on their back and sides is shorter.

Their fur keeps them warm in the cold. All that fluff makes this cat look bigger than it really is. Their fur also camouflages them while hunting. And hides them from predators such as foxes and eagles.

FACT The Pallas's cat's fur can be gray, tan, or orange with white tips.

#6 ALPACA

FACT FILE

- **ANIMAL GROUP:** Mammal
- **HABITATS:** Farms and ranches
- **AVERAGE SIZE:** A moped
- **DIET:** Herbivore

An alpaca's fur is woolly but light. It stays dry in rain or snow. An alpaca does not shed its fur like a dog or cat. It must be **sheared** every year.

If not, its fur becomes too hot. An adult alpaca can produce 5 to 8 pounds (2 to 4 kg) of fur per year. It can be made into warm clothing for people. Sweaters are the most common.

FACT Alpaca fur is often called fleece.

#5
BINTURONG
(bin-TOO-rong)

FACT FILE

ANIMAL GROUP: Mammal

HABITAT: Tropical forests

AVERAGE SIZE: A medium-sized dog

DIET: Omnivore

The binturong is also called a bearcat. This mammal spends most of its time in trees. The rainforest is wet. The binturong's long, shaggy coat helps keep its skin dry. Binturongs groom their coats like cats do.

They lick and nibble at their fur. They also have whiskers. You might smell a binturong before you see one. A **gland** under their tail makes them smell like buttered popcorn!

FACT A binturong looks like it is part bear and part cat. But it is not related to either.

#4 MUSK OX

FACT FILE

- **ANIMAL GROUP:** Mammal
- **HABITAT:** Arctic tundra
- **AVERAGE SIZE:** A couch
- **DIET:** Herbivore

Brrrr! It's cold! Musk oxen live out in the open. There are no trees. They have no protection from bad weather and freezing temperatures. Musk oxen owe their survival to their shaggy fur.

Their long fur almost reaches their feet. It is made up of two layers. The outer hairs are called guard hairs. Underneath is a warm layer of wool called qiviut (KEE-vee-uht).

FACT Winter for a musk ox typically reaches -40°F (-40°C) or colder! That is much colder than a freezer!

#3 SILKIE CHICKEN

FACT FILE

ANIMAL GROUP: Bird

HABITAT: Farms

AVERAGE SIZE: A basketball

DIET: Herbivore

Silkie chickens are *very* fluffy! They have feathers just like other birds. But Silkies' fur-like feathers are different. Most birds' feathers hook together.

They overlap and are smooth. Silkies' feathers do not hook together. Their soft feathers stick straight out! That's why Silkie chickens look like fluffy cotton balls.

FACT: Silkie chickens can be white, black, brown, gray, and even blue!

#2 ANGORA RABBIT

FACT FILE

- **ANIMAL GROUP:** Mammal
- **HABITAT:** Farms
- **AVERAGE SIZE:** A loaf of bread
- **DIET:** Herbivore

The Angora rabbit's fur is long, soft, and silky. It is one of the softest types of fur in the animal world. Each **strand** of fur is hollow, or empty.

Its fur traps heat to keep the rabbit warm. Some Angora rabbits do not shed, or **molt**. Their fur just keeps growing. They must be sheared every few months. Their fur is collected and used to make Angora wool.

FACT: Most Angora rabbits have white fur. But their fur can be many different colors.

#1 SEA OTTER

FACT FILE

ANIMAL GROUP: Mammal

HABITAT: Coastal waters

AVERAGE SIZE: A 7-year-old child

DIET: Carnivore

Which animal is the furriest? Sea otters have the thickest fur of any animal! And a lot of it. These mammals spend most of their time in the water. They don't have a layer of **blubber** like seals do.

To keep warm in cold water, they rely on their fur. They have a long, outer layer of guard hairs. These cover a second layer of softer fur. The soft fur traps air and heat next to their skin. The oily guard hairs keep water out.

FACT: Sea otters have a streamlined body. They can move quickly through water.

EYES
An otter has good eyesight, above and below the water.

EARS
Small ears close when the otter is underwater.

HIDDEN POCKETS
Baggy pockets of loose skin store food.

FACT: A sea otter can hold its breath for up to five minutes underwater.

SEA OTTER CLOSE-UP

PAWS
Five webbed fingers have sharp claws for holding food.

FUR
Two thick layers of short brown fur keep the otter warm and dry.

TAIL
Its long, muscular tail helps steer and swim.

SIZING THEM UP

There are many furry animals on Earth! Fur can be soft and fluffy. It can also be thick and woolly. Some animals use fur for protection. Some use fur to survive in harsh weather. Other animals use it to hide. Can you think of other furry animals? Try to create your own list!

GLOSSARY

blubber (BLUHB-ur) the layer of fat under the skin of a whale, seal, or other large marine mammal

camouflage (KAM-uh-flahzh) to disguise something so that it blends in with its surroundings

carnivore (KAHR-nuh-vor) an animal that eats meat

fur a soft covering on most mammals

gland an organ in the body that produces or releases natural chemicals

herbivore (HUR-buh-vor) an animal that only eats plants

invertebrate (in-VUR-tuh-brit) an animal without a backbone

mammal (MAM-uhl) a warm-blooded animal that has fur and usually gives birth to live babies

molt (mohlt) to lose old feathers or fur so that new ones can grow

omnivore (AHM-nuh-vor) an animal that eats both plants and meat

predator (PRED-uh-tur) an animal that lives by hunting other animals for food

shear (sheer) to cut the fur or fleece off a sheep or other animal

strand something that looks like a thread

tundra (TUHN-druh) a very cold area of northern Europe, Asia, and North America where there are no trees and the soil under the surface of the ground is always frozen

woolly (WUL-ee) of or relating to the soft, thick, and curly hair of animals such as sheep, llamas, and alpacas

INDEX

Page numbers in **bold** indicate images.

A
alpaca, 5, 16–17, **16–17**, 30
Angora rabbit, 5, 24–25, **24–25**
Arctic fox, **4**, 12–13, **12–13**
Arctic tundra animals. *See* Arctic fox; musk ox

B
bearcat. *See* binturong
binturong, 5, 18–19, **18–19**
birds. *See* Silkie chicken

C
carnivores. *See* Pallas's cat; sea otter

D
desert animals. *See* Pallas's cat

F
farm animals. *See* alpaca; Angora rabbit; Komondor; Silkie chicken

G
grassland animals. *See* Pallas's cat

H
herbivores. *See* alpaca; Angora rabbit; musk ox; Silkie chicken

I
invertebrates. *See* luna moth

K
Komondor, **4**, 6–9, **6–9**, 30
nickname, 8

L
luna moth, **4**, 10–11, **10–11**, 30

M
mammals. *See* alpaca; Angora rabbit; Arctic fox; binturong; Komondor; musk ox; Pallas's cat; sea otter
musk ox, **4**, 20–21, **20–21**

O
ocean animals. *See* sea otter
omnivores. *See* Arctic fox; binturong; Komondor

P
Pallas's cat, 5, 14–15, **14–15**

R
ranch animals. *See* alpaca

S
sea otter, 5, 26–29, **26–29**, 30
shrubland animals. *See* Pallas's cat
Silkie chicken, 5, 22–23, **22–23**, 30

T
tropical forest animals. *See* binturong

W
woodland animals. *See* luna moth

ABOUT THE AUTHOR

Brenna Maloney is the author of many books. She lives in Washington, DC, with her husband and two sons. If she had fur, she would want it to smell like popcorn, just like the binturong.